DATE DUE

JE 16 '99	JY 24 '00	JY 13 '07
JE 30 '99	JY 26 '00	DE 1 2 '07
OC 27 '99	JA 23 '02	
FE 07 '00	JY 1 4 '03	
JY 3 '00	AG 18 '04	

1. Books may be kept two weeks and may be renewed once for the same period, except 7 day books and magazines.

2. A fine is charged for each day a book is not returned according to the above rule. No book will be issued to any person incurring such a fine until it has been paid.

3. All injuries to books beyond reasonable wear and all losses shall be made good to the satisfaction of the Librarian.

4. Each borrower is held responsible for all books charged on his card and for all fines accruing on the same.

DEMCO

Good Mushrooms and Bad Toadstools

By Allan Fowler

Consultants

Linda Cornwell, Learning Resource Consultant,
Indiana Department of Education

Sharyn Fenwick, Elementary Science/Math Specialist,
Gustavus Adolphus College, St. Peter, Minnesota

Children's Press®
A Division of Grolier Publishing
New York   London   Hong Kong   Sydney
Danbury, Connecticut

Visit Children's Press® on the Internet at:
http://publishing.grolier.com

Designer: Herman Adler Design Group

Library of Congress Cataloging-in-Publication Data

Fowler, Allan.
    Good mushrooms and bad toadstools / by Allan Fowler.
      p. cm. — (Rookie read-about science)
    Includes index.
    Summary: Explains how mushrooms grow, which ones we eat, and
why some are safe to eat and some are not.
    ISBN 0-516-20808-X (lib. bdg.)   0-516-26363-3 (pbk.)
    1. Mushrooms—Juvenile literature. [1. Mushrooms.] I. Title. II. Series.
QK617.F64   1998   97-23255
579.6—dc21   CIP
                                      AC

Have you ever walked in a field, or in the woods, or on your lawn after a heavy rain and noticed mushrooms growing there? But you didn't see any mushrooms before it rained.

Can mushrooms really
spring up so quickly?

Yes, mushrooms seem to pop out of the ground in wet weather, as if by magic.

The mushroom you see is just part of a fungus. The rest of the fungus is a foot or so underground. Some fungi look like a tangle of white strands.

Plants need sunlight to make their own food and to grow. But most fungi can live without sunlight. They feed on dead plant and animal matter.

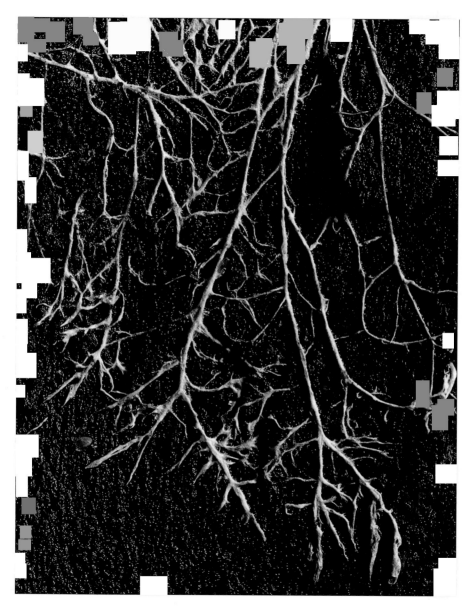

7

When the weather is mild
and moist, some types of
fungi send mushrooms
above ground.

A mushroom lasts just a few days. But the rest of the fungus can live for many years.

All mushrooms hold millions
of tiny spores. When the
spores fall off, they are
carried away by the wind.

If a spore lands in
a place with just the
right soil, moisture,
and temperature, it will
grow into a new fungus.

Only a very few spores
fall in the right place.
(If they all did, the
world would be covered
with fungi!)

There are three main groups of mushrooms. Each group is named for the location of its spores. The spores of sac mushrooms are found in wrinkly sacs on their surfaces.

In the pores on the
underside of a pore
mushroom is where
you'll find its spores.

The spores of a gill
mushroom are found in
gills on the underside of
the mushroom's cap.

Gills look a little like bicycle spokes.

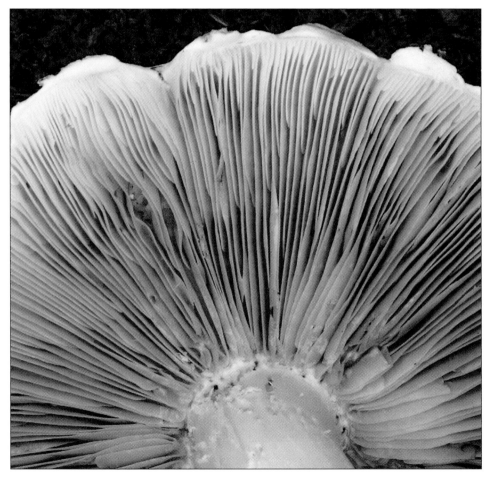

There are more than 3,000 different kinds of mushrooms. Some are more than a foot tall. Others may be less than an inch tall.

They come in many shapes
and colors.

This fly agaric mushroom is big and colorful, but you'd better not eat it.

You should never eat any mushroom you find growing wild.

Only an expert who knows all about mushrooms can tell which ones are safe to eat.

Some people use the word toadstool to describe mushrooms that taste bad or are poisonous. People can get sick and even die from eating toadstools.

The common meadow
mushroom is the kind
you usually eat. Meadow
mushrooms grow wild.

Farmers also grow them
on trays. These mushrooms
grow well in places that are
dark and damp, and neither
too cool nor too hot.

Morels are sac mushrooms. They look like spongy pinecones.

Farmers can't raise morels. They must be gathered in the woods.

Many people think morels are worth searching for because they taste so good.

A truffle is a kind of sac
mushroom that grows
completely underground.

In some countries, dogs and pigs are trained to sniff out truffles and dig them up.

Remember that only experts should pick mushrooms to eat.

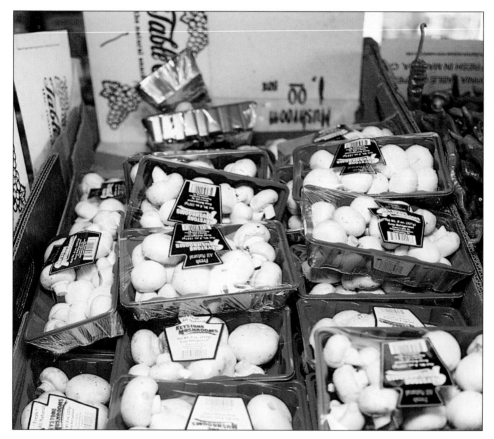

If you want to pick mushrooms, be sure to pick them at the supermarket— or off the top of a pizza!

Words You Know

mushrooms

cap

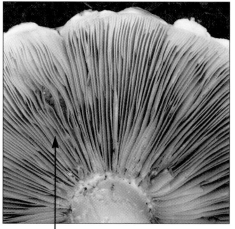

spores (on the gills)

fly agaric

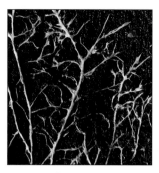

fungus

morel

toadstools

truffle

gill mushroom

meadow
mushrooms

pore
mushroom

sac mushroom

31

Index

cap, 14, 30

color, 17

eating, 19

experts, 19, 28

farmers, 23, 24

fly agaric mushroom, 18-19, 31

food, 6

fungi, 6-7, 8-9, 11, 31

gathering, 24, 27

gill mushrooms, 14-15, 31

gills, 14-15

ground, 5, 6, 26

growing, 4-5, 23

meadow mushrooms, 22-23, 31

morels, 24-25, 31

plants, 6

poisonous mushrooms, 20-21

pore mushrooms, 13, 31

reproduction, 10-11

sac mushrooms, 12, 24, 26, 31

safety, 19

size, 16

spores, 10-11, 12-14, 30

toadstools, 20-21, 31

truffles, 26-27, 31

weather, 3, 5, 8

wind, 10

About the Author

Allan Fowler is a freelance writer with a background in advertising. Born in New York, he now lives in Chicago and enjoys traveling.

Photo Credits